SCIENCE ESSENTIALS BIOLOGY

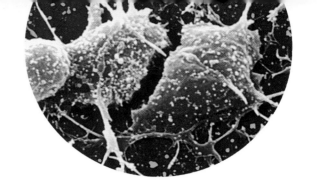

Cells and Life Processes

DENISE WALKER

EVANS

LONDON

© Evans Brothers Ltd 2006

Published by:
Evans Brothers
2a Portman Mansions
Chiltern Street
London W1U 6NR

Series editor:
Harriet Brown

Editor:
Katie Harker

Design:
Simon Morse

Illustrations:
Q2A Creative

Printed in China by
WKT Company Limited

British Library Cataloguing in
Publication Data

 Walker, Denise
   Cells and life processes. -
(Science essentials. Biology)
   1.Cells - Juvenile literature
2.Cytology - Juvenile
   literature
   I.Title
   571.6

ISBN-10: 0237530139
13-digit ISBN (from 1 January 2007)
978 0 23753013 6

Contents

Introduction

Living things are all around us – from tiny plants and tall trees, to microscopic bacteria and large animals. These living things all have one thing in common. They are made up of cells – the building blocks of life.

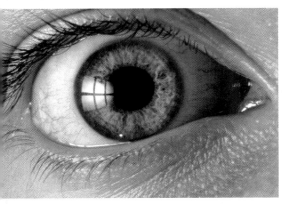

This book takes you on a journey to discover more about the wonderful world of cells and the processes that make life possible. Learn about what cells are made from and how they function. Discover ways in which cells work together to form larger organisms, and look at the differences between living and non-living objects. You can also find out about famous scientists, like Antony van Leeuwenhoek and Harold Urey. Learn how they used their skills to discover the existence of cells and to make judgements about the way in which life may have formed.

This book also contains feature boxes that will help you to unravel more about the mysteries of life processes. Test yourself on what you have learnt so far; investigate some of the concepts discussed; find out more key facts; and discover some of the scientific findings of the past and how these might be utilised in the future.

Cells are a vital part of our lives. Now you can understand more about the ways in which these tiny components make life possible.

DID YOU KNOW?

▶ Watch out for these boxes – they contain surprising and fascinating facts about cells and life processes.

TEST YOURSELF

▶ Use these boxes to see how much you've learnt. Try to answer the questions without looking at the book, but take a look if you are really stuck.

INVESTIGATE

▶ These boxes contain experiments that you can carry out at home. The equipment you will need is usually cheap and easy to find around the home.

TIME TRAVEL

These boxes contain scientific discoveries from the past and fascinating developments that pave the way for the advance of science in the future.

ANSWERS

At the end of this book on pages 46 and 47, you will find the answers to the questions from the 'Test yourself' and 'Investigate' boxes.

GLOSSARY

Words highlighted in **bold** are described in detail in the glossary on pages 46 and 47.

Living things

How do we know that something is alive?
In some cases it is very easy to tell. A hungry
tiger is obviously alive because it moves and
feeds. Tigers also give birth to their young.
However, to be classified as 'alive', organisms
(living things) need to demonstrate a number
of different behavioural patterns. In fact, we now
know that a vast range of biological processes
help the life forms on our planet to survive.

An **organism** is counted as living if it performs
each of the following processes:

M	Movement	Organisms move in order to avoid danger and to increase their chances of survival. Animals move away from predators and go in search of food. Plants do not move from place to place, but their roots grow in search of water and their leaves tilt towards the sunlight to produce food during **photosynthesis**.
R	Respiration	Organisms must **respire** so that they have the energy they need to grow and to carry out other life processes. Animals obtain this energy from a reaction between the food they eat and the oxygen they breathe (a process that releases carbon dioxide and water). Plants respire by changing oxygen from the air, and stored sugar in their leaves, into carbon dioxide and water.
S	Sensitivity	Organisms must respond to their environment in order to find the best possible conditions for life. Animals respond to the feeling of pain and they can also detect light through their eyes. Plants sense light and some plants can also respond to touch.

G	Growth	Organisms need to grow to reach their maximum potential and to eventually reproduce to make new living things. Plants continually grow throughout their lives, replacing leaves and shoots as time goes by. Animals grow in infancy until they reach a maximum adult size.
R	Reproduction	Organisms replace themselves through **reproduction**. This process is essential if species are to survive because organisms will always get old and die. Plants reproduce by making **seeds** that can grow into new plants. When animals reproduce, their babies grow and develop into adults.
E	Excretion	Organisms produce waste naturally when carrying out the processes of life. Excretion is a vital process that removes waste that would otherwise be poisonous. Plants excrete by storing waste in their leaves, which eventually fall off. Plants also release waste through openings in their leaves and through their roots. Animals get rid of their waste products through breathing, sweating and by passing urine or faeces.
N	Nutrition	Organisms need to absorb food: a fuel that is used to release energy for living. Green plants produce their food through a process called photosynthesis and they store this food in their leaves. Plant roots also absorb water and **nutrients**. Animals gain their food by eating plants or other animals – usually both.

Life processes are easy to recall if we remember the name 'MRS GREN'.

M	Movement
R	Respiration
S	Sensitivity
G	Growth
R	Reproduction
E	Excretion
N	Nutrition

TEST YOURSELF

▶ Research the characteristics of two organisms and list how they carry out the processes of life. For example, an emu (bird) and water lily (plant).

The building blocks of life

All living things are made from one or more cells. These tiny components perform the remarkable processes of life – everything, from mending wounds to reproducing new life, happens at cellular level. Many organisms are 'single-celled' (like bacteria). However, the living things that we generally see around us are 'multi-celled' (like humans, plants and animals). Whether single-celled or multi-celled, living things rely on the clever design of their cells for survival.

GOING SOLO

Single-celled organisms are able to carry out all the processes of life within one cell. They move by changing shape and some even contain light-sensitive chemicals that encourage them to move towards or away from a light source. Vital energy is obtained through the process of respiration (see page 9) and the organism reproduces by dividing into two equal cells. Some single-celled organisms (like bacteria) have been known to survive for millions of years, while others live for only a day.

TEAMWORK

The cells of multi-celled organisms are arranged so that they can work together to effectively carry out life processes. Some cells are particularly sensitive, like those situated in the eyes or the fingertips (where they are sensitive to light or pressure).

▲ Your eyes contain cells that are light-sensitive. Your pupil is small in bright conditions, but expands when it is dark to let more light in.

Likewise, plant cells can be sensitive to changes in light, heat and water levels.

Groups of cells work together to carry out particular actions. Muscle cells, for example, enable an animal to move. Cells also rely on each other for survival – gathering different chemicals and nutrients from each other. Multi-celled organisms grow because their cells are continually destroyed and replaced. The partnership of special 'sex' cells also enables these organisms to reproduce.

THE BREATH OF LIFE

Cells enable a single- or multi-celled organism to respire through a process called diffusion. Diffusion is caused by varying pressures on the surface of a cell encouraging substances to move into and out of the cell – creating a balance. Oxygen diffuses into a cell if there is more oxygen located on the outside of the cell (than on the inside). Likewise, carbon dioxide diffuses out of a cell if there is more carbon dioxide located on the inside of the cell (than on the outside). In multi-celled organisms, special 'transport' systems (like the blood), take these gases to other parts of the body to be used, or released as waste products.

The process of respiration converts an organism's food into energy. When you eat, your food is broken down and later enters the bloodstream via your intestines. The nutrients from your food travel to the cells of the body where they are needed most. There they react with oxygen (taken from the lungs) to release carbon dioxide, water and energy. Plants make their own food (glucose) during the process of photosynthesis. When glucose reacts with oxygen from the air, carbon dioxide, water and energy are produced.

WASTE DISPOSAL

Cells get rid of waste products through the process of excretion. This is because some substances, like carbon dioxide, can cause poisoning if they collect and remain in a cell. Waste products leave a cell by diffusion (see page 8). In multi-celled organisms, these products are transported to a suitable position where they can be removed. Animals excrete waste products by way of urine, faeces, sweat and the breathing out of carbon dioxide. In plants, waste is stored in dying leaves that fall off. Excess water, oxygen or carbon dioxide also diffuse through openings in the leaves or through the cell walls of roots.

ALL SHAPES AND SIZES

Most cells are so tiny that they cannot be seen with the naked eye. The smallest cell, a type of bacterium, measures 0.0001 millimetres in diameter, while the nerve cells that run down a giraffe's neck can be more than three metres in length! Thanks to technology we can now see the smallest cells for ourselves. We know, for example, that around 10,000 average-sized human cells could fit on the head of a pin. Cells also come in different shapes – some are squared or cubed, others are like columns or round like a doughnut.

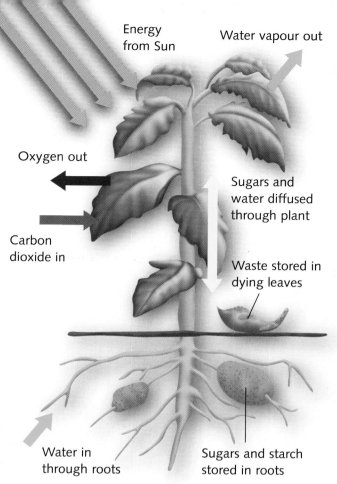

Energy from Sun

Water vapour out

Oxygen out

Carbon dioxide in

Sugars and water diffused through plant

Waste stored in dying leaves

Water in through roots

Sugars and starch stored in roots

▲ The processes of respiration, diffusion and excretion in a plant.

▼ Despite their differences, cells have many features in common.

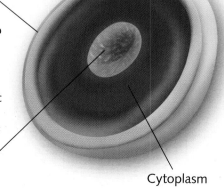

Cell membrane

The cell membrane makes up the outside of a cell and is similar in many ways to skin. The cell membrane allows substances to pass in and out of a cell. It can also control the shape of a cell.

Nucleus

Cytoplasm

The nucleus is the 'control centre' of a cell. It controls all of the processes that occur within an individual cell.

The cytoplasm makes up the bulk of a cell. Many cell processes occur within this thick, liquid-like substance.

TEST YOURSELF

▶ Make a list of the parts of some living organisms where you think there are sensitive cells. What are these cells sensitive to and what are they used for?

Animals and plants are sometimes referred to as 'eukaryotes'. The cells of these organisms have a nucleus. However, some single-celled organisms have no nucleus at all. These organisms are known as 'prokaryotes' (for example, bacteria). Before we discuss prokaryotes, let's take a closer look at the structure of plant and animal cells.

A TYPICAL ANIMAL CELL

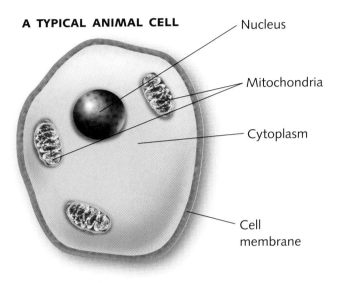

Approximately x 5,000 magnification.

ANIMAL CELLS

Look at the features of this animal cell. Notice that in this example the nucleus is found near the centre of the cell and is the largest of the cell components. The tiny rod-like structures in the cytoplasm are called 'mitochondria'. These are present in the cytoplasm of most animal and plant cells and provide the energy a cell needs to carry out life processes. Some cells have three or four mitochondria but cells that need more energy can have several thousands. The cell membrane looks like it is holding all the parts of the cell together and giving the cell some kind of shape. In other animal cells the nucleus, cytoplasm, mitochondria and cell membrane may be found in slightly different positions.

PLANT CELLS

Plant cells have additional features – a cell wall, vacuole and chloroplasts. They need these extra features to carry out the processes of life. Notice here that the nucleus, cytoplasm, mitochondria and cell membrane are also in different positions to those found in the illustrated animal cell.

A TYPICAL PLANT CELL

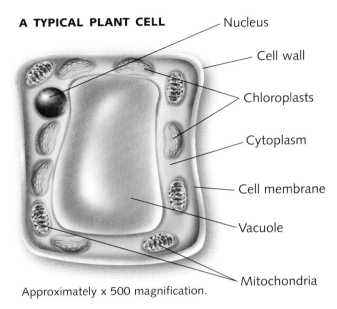

Approximately x 500 magnification.

In plants, the cell wall covers the cell membrane and provides strength to support the plant. Animals do not need this feature because they use a skeleton or a shell, for example, to support them. Plant cells also have a **vacuole**, which contains the 'cell sap'. Because plants don't move from place to place, like animals, they need to be able to store nutrients for times when food is scarce. The cell sap gathers and stores vital nutrients. Animal cells have no need for a vacuole – instead of storing food, animals get the nutrients they need by eating other organisms.

When the plant cell takes in water, the vacuole fills and begins to swell. This exerts pressure onto the cell wall and the whole cell becomes **turgid**.

Plants need water so that they can stay supported. This is why a plant wilts if it is left in the heat of the Sun. On warm days, water diffuses out of the plant cell and evaporates from the leaves. Because this reduces the pressure on the cell wall, the cell becomes **flaccid**. If this happens to a number of cells, the plant begins to droop.

Lastly, and importantly, plant cells contain small green 'bodies' called chloroplasts. These are similar to mitochondria but are found only in plant cells. Chloroplasts contain a substance called chlorophyll that plants use to convert sunlight into usable energy through the process of photosynthesis. Animals don't use photosynthesis to gain food, so they have no need for chloroplasts.

Cell components	Animal cells	Plant cells
Nucleus	✔	✔
Cell membrane	✔	✔
Cell wall		✔
Cytoplasm	✔	✔
Mitochondria	✔	✔
Vacuole		✔
Chloroplasts		✔

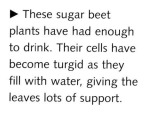

Flaccid cell

▲ The cells of these thirsty sugar beet plants have lost water in the heat. As the cells become flaccid there is less internal support and the plants begin to wilt.

Turgid cell

► These sugar beet plants have had enough to drink. Their cells have become turgid as they fill with water, giving the leaves lots of support.

3

A closer inspection

Most cells are so small that they cannot be seen with the naked eye. However, in the 1600s, the development of the microscope enabled scientists to uncover the mysteries of cellular life. Plant cells are the largest of all (about one tenth of a millimetre in size) and were the first to be discovered. Most animal cells are about a tenth of this size. Thanks to staggering advances in microscopy we are now able to see the tiny components that are responsible for sustaining life.

LIGHT MICROSCOPY

In the eyepiece of a light microscope there is a lens which is usually of x 10 magnification. If you look at an object through the eyepiece lens, it appears ten times bigger than it actually is in real life.

At the bottom of the microscope is a light source (or a mirror to reflect light), which allows the viewer to see the sample. The sample is placed for viewing on the stage, above which there are three additional lenses of different sizes (called 'objective lenses'). The smallest lens might be x 10 magnification. This lens would make the sample appear to be 100 times larger than it actually is (10 x 10). The largest lens is usually x 40 magnification – magnifying the sample to 400 times its actual size (10 x 40).

A LIGHT MICROSCOPE

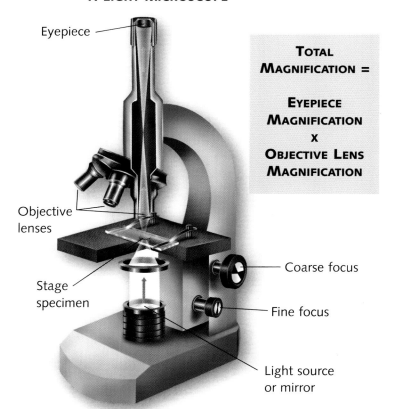

Eyepiece

Objective lenses

Stage specimen

Coarse focus

Fine focus

Light source or mirror

TOTAL MAGNIFICATION =

EYEPIECE MAGNIFICATION x OBJECTIVE LENS MAGNIFICATION

INVESTIGATE

▶ You can set up a light microscope to see cells for yourself. A simple sample could be a small slice of onion.

(1) If your microscope has a mirror, tilt it to increase the amount of light that passes through the microscope. This will appear as the brightest arrangement.
(2) Place the slide sample onto the stage and clip it into position.
(3) Turn the objective lenses so that the smallest lens is in position first.
(4) Use the coarse focus knob to bring the sample into view. Sharpen the image using the fine focus knob.
(5) Turn the objective lenses so that the next largest is now in position.
(6) Use the fine focus knob to bring the view back into a sharp picture.
(7) Repeat the last two steps for the largest objective lens.
What can you see?

ELECTRON MICROSCOPY

Some samples, like tiny bacterium, are too small to be seen by a light microscope, and even the largest magnifying lens does not make them visible to the human eye. However, smaller samples can now be viewed using an instrument called an electron microscope. This instrument works in the same way as a light microscope, but a focused beam of electrons is used instead of light to 'see through' the sample. The most powerful electron microscopes are capable of showing images 500,000 times larger than they actually are.

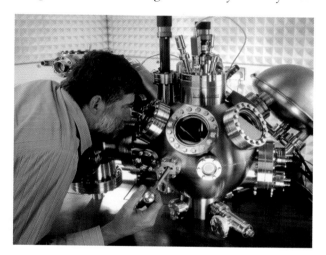

▲ Electron microscopes are used to view small cells.

INVESTIGATE

▶ Using this picture taken by a light microscope, measure the dimensions of one onion cell and calculate the real size using the magnification given.

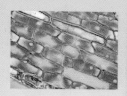

x 60

▶ Using this picture taken by an electron microscope, measure the dimensions of the radiolarian cell and calculate the real size using the magnification given.

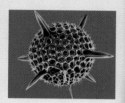

x 664

MICROSCOPE TECHNOLOGY

Microscopes are getting better all the time. In the 1980s, a group of scientists invented what is known as a 'scanning tunnelling microscope'. This invention enabled scientists to see the individual atoms on the surface of an object for the first time. The microscope uses special techniques to achieve clear images of very small detail and has one major advantage – instead of preparing slide samples, scientists can study objects in their natural environment. Developments in microscope technology have been building on this invention.

Today, the most powerful microscopes have enabled us to discover organisms that are around 40 millionths of a centimetre wide. These organisms, called 'nanobacteria', are so tiny that their discovery has changed previous assumptions about how small an organism can be to contain the mechanisms for life.

TIME TRAVEL: DISCOVERIES OF THE PAST

The Dutchman, Antony van Leeuwenhoek (below) made some of the most important discoveries in the history of cellular biology in the 1600s, when he made over 500 magnifying lenses. Leeuwenhoek found that his 'microscopes' could magnify objects to approximately 200 times their actual size. Leeuwenhoek's careful observations uncovered the existence of many microscopic organisms – such as bacteria and blood cells – helping to form the basis of modern biology. Later that century, the British scientist Robert Hooke confirmed Leeuwenhoek's work and improved the design of his lenses. Hooke developed the first light (or 'compound') microscope and was also the first person to use the term 'cell'.

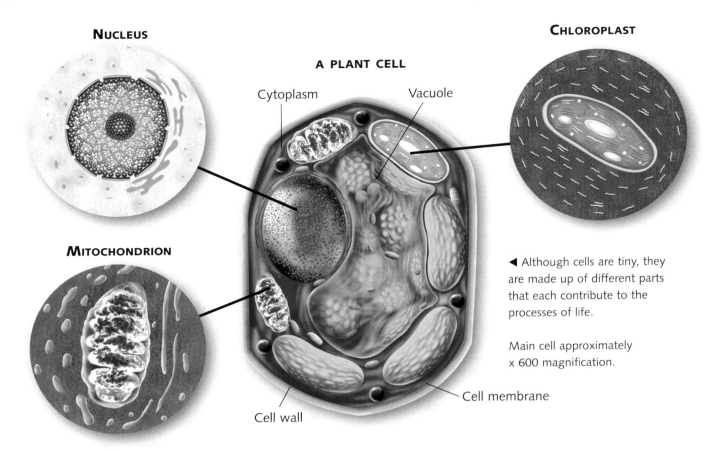

NUCLEUS

A PLANT CELL

Cytoplasm

Vacuole

CHLOROPLAST

MITOCHONDRION

◀ Although cells are tiny, they are made up of different parts that each contribute to the processes of life.

Main cell approximately x 600 magnification.

Cell membrane

Cell wall

A closer examination of cell structure has shown scientists that a cell's design enables it to carry out specific tasks – such as breaking down glucose for energy, building cell walls and reproducing. In fact, each part of a cell contributes to the processes of life in its own unique way.

DID YOU KNOW?

▶ Animals that eat raw plants need special chemicals, called enzymes, to be able to digest the very tough material found in the cell wall of plants. This material is called 'cellulose'. Because humans no longer have these enzymes they are unable to break down cellulose (or 'fibre'). Instead, cellulose passes through the body as a waste product.

NUCLEUS

In eukaryotes, like animals and plants, the nucleus of a cell controls all of the cell's actions – from when it should respire to when it should reproduce or die. Most important of all, the nucleus contains the inherited information that is individual to each organism. This information is stored in a special molecule in the nucleus, called **DNA** (deoxyribonucleic acid). All of our cells contain the same **genetic** (inherited) information – this is what makes it possible to identify a person from just one cell, a technique often used in criminal cases.

CYTOPLASM

The cytoplasm forms the bulk of the cell and acts as a bed in which to place other cell components. The cytoplasm is a thick, gel-like liquid that allows other substances to pass through it from either outside or inside the cell. Proteins, called '**enzymes**', fill the cytoplasm and are used by the cell to grow, reproduce and to create energy.

CELL MEMBRANE

The cell membrane is the outside layer of a cell. It gives the cell shape and holds it together while substances move in and out of the cell. The cell membrane can be permeable, semi-permeable or impermeable. A cell membrane that is permeable will allow all substances into and out of the cell. A cell membrane that is semi-permeable will only allow certain substances through – this might depend on something like the size of the substance (see page 16). A cell membrane that is impermeable will not allow any substances through.

CELL WALL

The cell wall of a plant cell is made from a very hard material called cellulose. Cell walls are used to keep the plant supported. They also influence the shape of the plant and protect the cells from harmful bacteria and viruses.

VACUOLE

This round fluid-filled sack is used to store nutrients and to release waste products. The vacuole also acts like a 'water reservoir' keeping the plant cell hydrated and turgid (see page 10).

TEST YOURSELF

▶ What features do plant cells have that animal cells don't have? What would happen to a plant if it didn't have these extra features?

MITOCHONDRIA

Mitochondria provide cells with the energy they need to move, divide and to carry out chemical reactions. Organs or tissues that need lots of energy to work (such as the heart or the skeletal muscles) have cells containing several thousand mitochondria. Cells that do not require as much energy may only have three or four.

CHLOROPLASTS

A typical plant cell might contain as many as 50 chloroplasts. These disc-like structures are found in all plant cells that lie above the ground. They use the energy of the Sun to make food for the plant. Chloroplasts are also responsible for giving leaves their green colour.

TIME TRAVEL: DISCOVERIES OF THE PAST

Scientists think that over billions of years ago, mitochondria and chloroplasts were actually bacteria. They believe that eukaryotes evolved by forming a relationship with prokaryotes (see page 10). Prokaryotes engulfed and fed bacteria in return for some of the bacteria's energy. Eventually the bacteria no longer needed to live independently and became a cell component. Although this view was ignored for most of the 1900s, the theory is now generally accepted across the scientific community. Scientists have found that mitochondria and chloroplasts contain their own genetic material and have a double membrane (like the DNA and membrane of a bacterium). This computer-generated image of a mitochondrion clearly shows the smooth outer membrane and the folded inner membrane. Mitochondria are thought to have developed from 'aerobic bacteria', which use oxygen to produce energy, while chloroplasts are thought to have originated from 'cyanobacteria', which produce energy via photosynthesis.

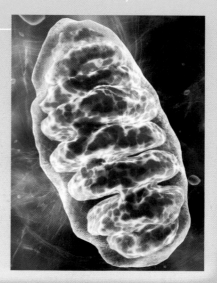

Although all cells contain key components, cell structure can vary between different types of cells. In particular, variations in the size of a cell and the type of cell membrane that it has can cause different cellular reactions.

CELL MEMBRANE

Cell membranes are responsible for allowing materials (that cells need) to pass into the cell, and materials (that cells do not want) to pass out. Cells must be careful to distinguish between 'useful' substances and 'waste' products, but how do they manage this process?

Cell membranes are made from fatty layers that contain many small holes, called 'pores', in their surface. These allow substances to pass through depending on:

a) the size of the substance.

Substances that are too large cannot pass through the pores in the cell membrane.

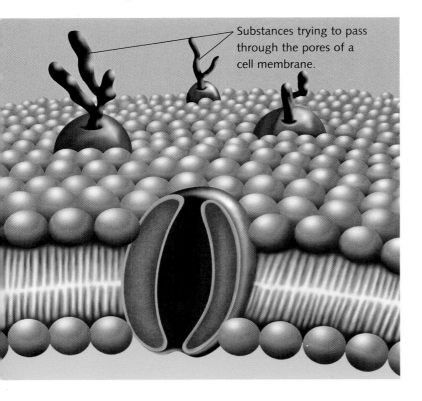

Substances trying to pass through the pores of a cell membrane.

b) whether the substance has an 'electrical charge' that causes it to be attracted to the cell.

Some pores in the cell membrane have a positive or negative electrical charge. If a substance with an opposite charge comes into contact with the cell it is attracted to the cell membrane and passes through.

c) the amount of substance on each side of the cell membrane.

If there is a small amount of substance on one side of the membrane, the substance can pass through by the process of diffusion (see page 8).

ACTIVE AND PASSIVE TRANSPORT

When substances pass through a cell membrane by diffusion, the movement is known as 'passive transport'. Rather like a siphon transporting water, diffusion causes substances to move between cell areas with differing concentrations. However, sometimes, cells require 'active transport' if they need to move particularly important substances. Here, the action is more like a water pump because the cell uses energy to transport the material from low to high concentrations.

FIT TO BURST!

Plant and animal cell membranes help to control the substances that move into and out of a cell. The process of diffusion ensures that there is an equal concentration of substances on either side of the cell membrane. The small pores of the

◄ A semi-permeable cell membrane will only allow certain substances to pass through. Approximately x 12,000 magnification.

membrane also restrict the type of molecule that can pass through. That said, animal cells do not have any control about the amount of liquid that can enter them – in watery solutions, animal cells can swell up and burst! Animals have to excrete excess water to prevent this from happening. In humans and some animals, kidneys regulate the amount of water in the blood. In contrast, plant cells are protected by a cell wall – if too much water enters a plant cell it becomes turgid but does not burst (see page 10).

▲ Animal cells can burst if they absorb too much liquid. Humans and some animals excrete water, in the form of urine, to prevent this from happening.

CELL SIZE

Cells are microscopic but their size varies. There are two aspects of cell size: surface area and volume.

Imagine a cube-shaped cell with edges measuring one centimetre.

The volume of the cell is $1 \times 1 \times 1 = 1^3 = 1\,cm^3$. Each face of the 'cell' is one centimetre squared and there are six of these. This means that the surface area of the cell is $6\,cm^2$. The surface area to volume ratio is 6:1.
Now, imagine another cube-shaped cell with edges measuring two centimetres.

Volume $= 2 \times 2 \times 2 = 8\,cm^3$
Surface area $= 2 \times 2 \times 6 = 24\,cm^3$
Surface area to volume ratio $= 24:8 = 3:1$

As cells grow, their volume increases more than their surface area. At some point, the surface area of a cell will be too small to provide its volume with the nutrients it needs to survive. Large cells need more oxygen and food for survival, and their relatively small surface area cannot provide this. Rather than grow bigger, a cell will divide into two.

TEST YOURSELF

▶ For each of the following sized cells, calculate the 'surface area to volume ratio'.

Which cell would find it easiest to satisfy its food and oxygen needs?

(1) 2 x 3 x 4 cm

(2) 3 x 3 x 3 cm

(3) 1 x 1 x 2 cm

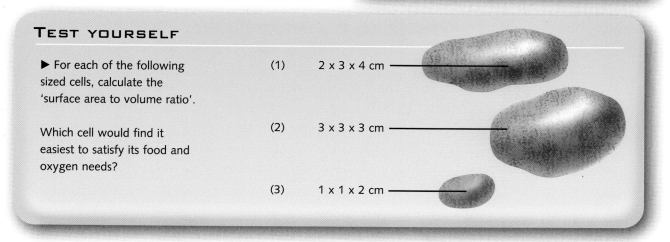

4

Is it alive?

Some unusual beings, like amoebas and bacteria, contribute to the amazing diversity of life on Earth. A closer inspection of these organisms reveals that what may initially seem to be a lifeless object is very much alive and kicking.

SINGLE-CELLED ORGANISMS

The living organisms that we see around us are made from thousands of billions of microscopic cells. But some organisms are clever enough to be able to carry out the processes of life in just one cell (see page 8).

AMOEBAS

Amoebas are **aquatic** single-celled organisms that can be found all over the world in both fresh and salt water sources, as well as in water found in the soil. Amoebas can be seen under a light microscope and have no fixed shape. Amoebas are classified as living because:

▶ An amoeba can move by changing shape and growing **tentacles** in one direction. Amoebas can grow much bigger than most single-celled organisms – some are up to five millimetres long.

▶ An amoeba can detect and move towards nearby food sources. Amoebas 'eat' their food by releasing a chemical that causes the food to break down, before absorbing it by diffusion.

▶ Oxygen enters an amoeba by diffusion and combines with food to release energy. The waste products of an amoeba also pass into the surrounding water by diffusion.

▶ An amoeba can reproduce by splitting into two identical individuals.

◀ Amoebas eat by 'engulfing' their food. They move towards their food and surround it, before eventually absorbing it into the cell.

Artwork x 125 magnification.

Food

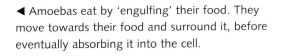

BACTERIA

Bacteria are single, self-contained living cells but they are unusual because they don't have a proper nucleus – the 'control centre' of a cell. Instead of a nucleus, bacteria have strands of DNA that carry all the information that the cell needs to function (see page 24).

VIRUSES

Viruses are not strictly classified as 'cells' and consist of little more than protein and DNA. Viruses are therefore not themselves alive, but carry out the processes of life by hijacking the machinery of a living cell. Viruses infect a **host cell** with their own genetic material which instructs the cell to produce more viruses (see page 26).

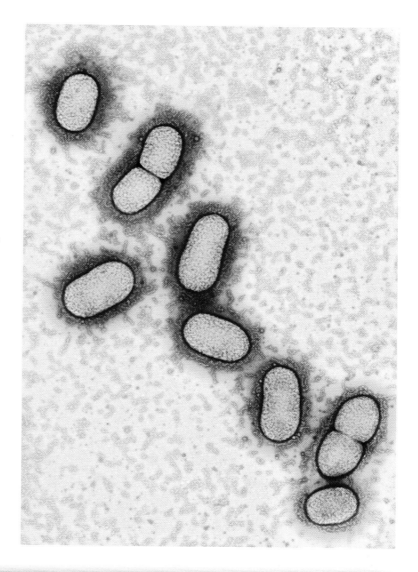

▶ Oral bacteria viewed under an electron microscope. This type of bacteria can cause gum disease and mouth ulcers. Notice how two of the bacteria are dividing (upper left and lower right).
Microscopic image x 18,000 magnification.

TEST YOURSELF

▶ For each of the following organisms, use the information provided to decide which characteristics indicate that the object is a living thing:

Barnacles

These organisms live on rocks or the bottom of boats. The larvae of barnacles are like shrimps and swim freely in water, but once they attach to a hard surface, they form an outer shell and rarely move. When they are submerged in water, barnacles tend to extend their feathery legs from the shell to gather plankton from water for their food.

Venus Flytrap

This plant feeds on animal life. It traps insects that land on the plant's leaves, by shutting its leaves together.

For hundreds of years, scientists have been trying to copy the living organisms that are all around us. Today, this scientific discipline (called 'artificial life') attempts to create living things using robots, computers or chemical techniques. The construction of living organisms from non-living parts has been one of the most ambitious tasks that scientists have ever set themselves.

Artificial life is forcing many people to rethink their definition of 'life'. The study currently takes two forms – the creation of life from nature's own building blocks (cells) and the simulation of life using computers and robots.

Vaucanson's duck

In 1738, a French engineer called Jacques Vaucanson, built a mechanical duck out of 30 moving levers and hundreds of interlocking parts. To an audience, the duck appeared to be very lifelike as it moved its wings, sat up, sat down, cleaned itself and drank water. The duck also seemed to be able to eat, digest and excrete waste products. However, such complicated life processes were just visual illusions.

In the 1700s, some people thought that life was a mechanical process while others believed that the mystery of life would always lie beyond our

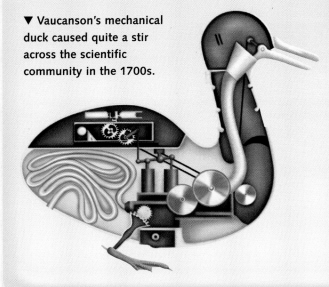

▼ Vaucanson's mechanical duck caused quite a stir across the scientific community in the 1700s.

reach. It was never considered that a clockwork duck could actually be alive, but Vaucanson's work led followers of the 'mechanical' view to believe that one day it might be possible to produce an artificial living creature. The duck also provided scientists with a good reason to continue with their studies – people paid a lot of money to see the show!

Artificial intelligence

The human brain and the modern day computer have many features in common. They are both capable of carrying out a set of commands (that are learnt or programmed) and they can both be active around the clock. In this research area, scientists believe that they can create intelligence artificially – but can a computer be programmed to act like a human brain?

▲ Modern computers are beginning to imitate the brain's ability to learn from trial and error.

Progress in artificial intelligence was brought to the public's attention in the 1990s with the advancement of chess-playing computer programmes. In 1990, former chess world champion, Anatoly Karpov, was beaten by the German computer 'Mephisto-Portrose' and in 1996, reigning chess-champion, Gary Kasparov, lost to IBM's computer 'Deep Thought'. These two intelligent thinkers just couldn't overcome the power and speed of the computer's processing technology.

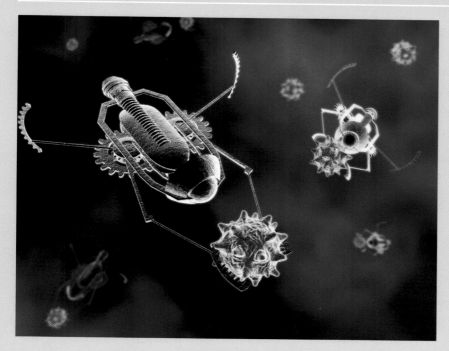

◄ In the future, tiny robots could be developed to treat diseases in a different way. These illustrated robots are shown attacking harmful bacteria cells. Others could be used to destroy cancer cells or to remove clots in blood vessels.

Approximately
x 600 magnification.

THE ROBOT REVOLUTION

In 2004, a team of British researchers reported that they had created a 'robot scientist' that could design experiments and evaluate results – bad news for young researchers seeking employment! But while this 'robot scientist' performed well in the laboratory it could only observe what it was programmed to find. A robot may work quickly and accurately, but unlike human scientists, it is unable to notice the unexpected or make new discoveries. Although complex behaviour is one characteristic of living organisms, robots fail to demonstrate other key processes of life.

Computer scientists have now gone one step further by developing computers that can carry out actions that they have not been programmed to perform. This is possible with computers that have a feature called a 'neural net' – a network that imitates the brain's ability to sort out patterns and learn from trial and error. So how far do we think that computer technology will go in its attempt to imitate living organisms? Already, Japanese designers have created robots that are capable of domestic chores, like answering the door and serving prepared drinks to their owners. Some

hospitals in the USA and the UK have begun to use 'robot' doctors. These robots are linked to a real-life doctor, but carry out bedside consultations in their absence. But will robots ever be able to carry out all life processes?

▶ Robots can move, but they are powered electrically so have no need to respire to release energy. Robots don't require food to make energy and they don't produce or excrete waste products.
▶ Some robots are sensitive to objects that are in their path and move to avoid them, while others can also respond to light and sound signals.
▶ Robots are man-made and they neither have the need nor the ability to reproduce. Robots are also made to an ideal size and have no need to grow.

CREATING LIFE

Ever since scientists have uncovered the workings of a living cell and learnt more about the genetic instructions that control a cell, they have been trying to search for ways in which life might be artificially created. Turn to page 44 to find out more about the work of scientists trying to create living organisms from scratch – and their ultimate quest to uncover the origins of life.

5

The single life

Single-celled organisms are classified as living because they perform the processes of life within one cell. These organisms have been the subject of much scientific research. Amoebas, for example, can be easily kept in a laboratory and are commonly used to investigate cell structure and function. Despite having only one cell to work with, these compact life forms are incredible beings.

AMOEBAS

ON THE MOVE

Amoebas can move because they can change shape and grow tentacles in one direction. This process is called 'cytoplasmic streaming' as the cytoplasm of the cell flows in one direction all at the same time. You can see the movement of cytoplasmic streaming under a light microscope. Amoebas form extensions (that look like arms) on their outer surface into which the cytoplasm

flows. These 'arms' become bigger as the cytoplasm gradually flows into them. Eventually the arms become so big that the bulk of the cell has effectively moved to a new position. The driving force behind this movement is not fully understood, but it is thought that as cytoplasm flows in one direction, it is being dragged from an opposite corner of the cell.

KEEPING ALIVE

Amoebas are sensitive organisms because they can move towards food and away from danger. Scientists think that amoebas are able to move because they can detect changing concentrations of chemicals in the water in which they live.

Amoebas need oxygen and food to respire and this occurs through the process of diffusion. An amoeba must have a high 'surface area to volume ratio' in order to be able to get enough food and oxygen into its cell (see page 17). Amoebas will only grow to a certain size before they divide and reproduce. If an amoeba grew too big its small surface area to volume ratio would cause it to starve.

Amoebas move towards and around their food so that they eventually engulf it. Chemicals (called 'enzymes') are released to help the amoeba to break the food down into more manageable parts

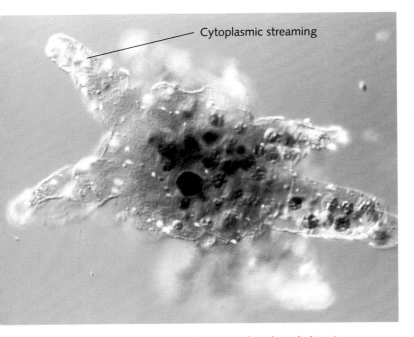

Cytoplasmic streaming

▲ A moving amoeba viewed under a light microscope (x 170 magnification). Notice the cytoplasmic streaming as parts of the organism are extended.

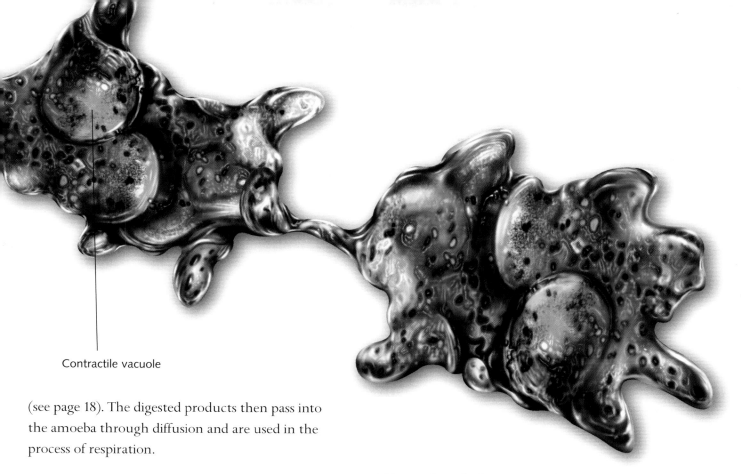

Contractile vacuole

(see page 18). The digested products then pass into the amoeba through diffusion and are used in the process of respiration.

Amoebas have developed an efficient system of getting rid of waste substances and excess water. Amoebas are aquatic organisms so they constantly have water entering their cell. To prevent them from bursting, amoebas contain a special structure called a 'contractile vacuole'. As water enters the cell, this vacuole fills up and begins to move to the surface of the amoeba. When the vacuole reaches the cell surface, it bursts and excess water leaves the cell. Waste products also leave the cell by diffusion.

CREATING NEW LIFE

Amoebas reproduce by splitting into two identical cells. When they become too big to remain as one organism the parent cell splits into two approximately equal parts, which scientists call 'daughter' cells. This method of reproduction is called **binary fission** and is a form of **asexual** reproduction.

▲ This amoeba is dividing into two identical cells because it has grown too large to be able to sustain itself. Notice the contractile vacuole which is used to expel excess water. Artwork x 170 magnification.

CLEVER CELLS

Scientists in Japan have revealed that slime mould (a single-celled organism similar to amoeba) exhibits some form of primitive intelligence. In their study, pieces of slime mould were encouraged to follow a 30 cm² maze with the reward of food at the end of the puzzle. Although slime mould usually moves to fill up available space, when two pieces of food were placed at separate exits of the maze, the organism adopted the shortest possible route and squeezed its body to reach both food prizes. When it comes to food, it seems that even lower life forms can find a way to get their sustenance!

BACTERIA

Bacteria live in a variety of diverse environments, from inside humans to woodland soil. Washing your hands and keeping your house clean can prevent the spread of bacteria. Bacteria usually join together and attach themselves to a surface. These groups are called 'biofilm' communities and can be found in many everyday environments, from the plughole of a sink to the plaque around your teeth!

Bacteria live in our bodies all the time and are usually harmless – some even help with vital processes like the digestion of our food. Sometimes, however, bacterial infections can make us unwell. Food poisoning, tetanus and tuberculosis are all illnesses caused by bacteria. But whilst bacteria can cause us harm, they are also essential components of our ecosystem – breaking down waste material into a form that plants can use for nourishment. Bacteria can also

be used to make antibiotics (medicines that help your body to fight harmful bacteria) and as a vital ingredient in food production (see page 28).

Bacteria adopt a variety of shapes and are so small that they can only be seen under a very high-powered microscope. Bacteria have no nucleus but they contain strands of DNA that holds all the information that the cell needs. In other cells, DNA is usually found in the nucleus.

(see page 28)

TIME TRAVEL: DISCOVERIES OF THE PAST

In 1993, scientists discovered the largest known bacterium. At 0.5 millimetres long, this was the first bacterium to be visible without a microscope and was found to live in the intestine of the Red Sea surgeon fish. This discovery led scientists to rethink their belief that bacteria had a critical size above which they would be deprived of vital nutrients.

SPECIAL FEATURES OF BACTERIA CELLS

Bacteria are capable of movement as many have hair strands (called flagella) which beat to propel the cell forward. Scientists often marvel at the clever design of flagella – these little 'propellors' that rotate to move the cell forward are rather like the machines that a human would have created. The flagella cause movement but scientists also think the hairs provide the cell with a degree of sensitivity.

A BACTERIUM WITH FLAGELLA

DNA

Cytoplasm

Cell wall

Flagella

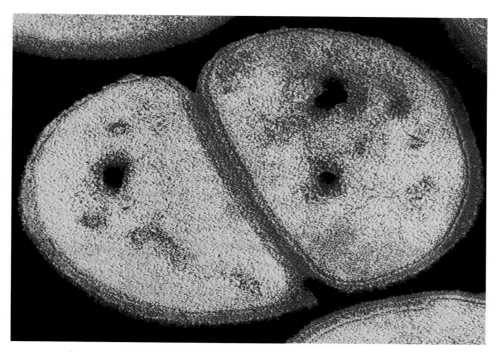

◄ This bacterium, viewed under an electron microscope (x 105,000 magnification) is dividing using binary fission. The bacterium has no flagella but moves by gliding across a surface.

Like amoebas, bacteria only grow to a certain size before they divide and reproduce using binary fission. Bacteria reproduce very fast and large populations can soon build up. Some bacteria divide every 20 minutes. That means that in just five hours, one bacterium can trigger the reproduction of 32,000 new bacteria cells! This can be alarming if the bacteria cause disease; the infection is likely to spread very rapidly.

Like most organisms, bacteria need the correct environmental conditions in which to live. Bacteria need water, a food supply and a source of energy to trigger chemical reactions. Some bacteria require light, while others need oxygen. More recently, however, scientists have discovered a group of organisms known as 'extremophiles', that thrive in conditions that had previously been thought to be too hot, too acidic, too dark or too oxygen-deprived for life to survive. Ice samples taken from Arctic glaciers and samples from acid hot springs and volcanic vents have shown that, even in the most extreme environments, bacteria are still thriving. These discoveries keep changing our views about the nature of bacteria.

▼ In hot springs, like this thermal pool at Yellowstone Park, USA, bacteria are thriving.

VIRUSES

Viruses are not cells, but they carry out the processes of life by manipulating another living cell. Some viruses attach to a host without causing harm, while others have a damaging effect. Like bacteria, viruses can have very different shapes and structures. Most can only be seen under an electron microscope.

SPECIAL FEATURES OF VIRUSES

Many viruses have spikes that protrude from their surface. These spikes are capable of recognising host cells when they come into contact – suggesting that viruses are capable of sensitivity.

▼ AIDS is caused by the human immunodeficiency virus (HIV). The surface knobs (shown in yellow) are used to attach the virus to a host cell. HIV attacks white blood cells which play an important role in the immune system. Artwork showing the virus at x 840,000 magnification.

Viruses are 'parasitic'. They can feed on and destroy your body's cells, or produce chemicals that are poisonous to your cells. Viruses also use your cells to reproduce. When a virus invades a cell it injects its own genetic information into the cytoplasm of the host cell. This process instructs the cell to produce lots of new viruses – eventually so many are produced that the host cell bursts to release them and is destroyed in the process. This event can cause minor irritations like sneezing and coughing and can make you feel unwell because the virus is interfering with the workings of your body. Viral infections also include more serious diseases like measles and polio.

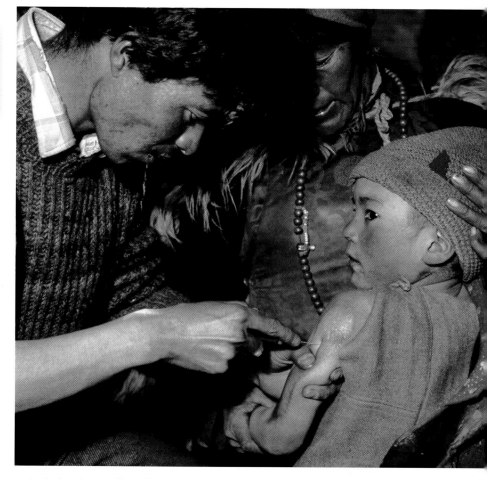

▲ India has been affected by a number of measles outbreaks in recent years. Doctors have tried to prevent the virus from spreading by vaccinating adults and children.

Although bacteria are capable of causing harm to other living organisms, many bacteria cells are actually useful to us. Over the years, scientists have developed techniques that use the features of bacteria in many important areas of our lives.

BACTERIA IN THE ENVIRONMENT

Large communities of bacteria are found in soil where they are responsible for breaking down many important nutrients, such as nitrogen, into a form that can be reused by plants and other organisms.

▼ **Bacteria help to decompose the plant matter on this forest floor, creating vital nutrients for other plant life.**

Recently, scientists have also found bacteria living in clouds. They believe that these bacteria are helping to regulate the Earth's surface temperature – by encouraging the formation of clouds that reflect solar radiation during the day and keep warmth in at night. It is thought that the bacteria are also making compounds that are used in the production of ozone, therefore protecting against the Sun's powerful rays.

Bacteria have uses in the control of pollution too – such as cleaning up waste dumps or landfill sites. Sometimes methane gas is added to the soil at a dump to encourage bacteria (that feed on methane gas) to grow. As the bacteria multiply they begin to break down pollutants into harmless substances. As we advance technologically, many new waste products are being introduced into the environment that cannot be broken down. However, some scientists believe that by genetically modifying bacteria we will be able to continue to clean up the environment effectively.

BACTERIA IN FOOD PRODUCTION

Many aspects of food technology involve the use of bacteria. Traditionally, bacteria have been used in bread making, brewing and the production of cheese and yoghurt. Today, bacteria are also used in the production of soy sauce and bean curd.

Cheese is made from milk. If bacteria are added to milk they feed on lactose (milk sugar) which forms lactic acid and converts the milk into a solid and a liquid part called 'curds' and 'whey'. The curds are pressed to remove the water, and other bacteria may be added for flavour (for example, in blue cheese like Stilton). A substance called 'rennin' is also added to help the bacteria convert the milk to curds and whey. In the past, rennin was obtained from the stomachs of young cattle. It can now be made by yet another bacterium and this gives rise to vegetarian cheese.

▲ **Bacteria has been used to make this cheese and to give it flavour. Most supermarket cheeses are now produced using a vegetarian source of rennin.**

BACTERIA IN MEDICINE

Many of our medicines have traditionally been extracted from sources such as plant materials. Because there may be a limited supply of such sources on Earth (making certain medicines more

expensive and perhaps unavailable), biologists and other scientists have developed a means of producing medical treatments made from bacteria. For example, diabetes is a disease that is treated with a hormone called insulin, which is now derived from bacteria.

Diabetes is a disorder in which people are unable to produce enough insulin (a substance that controls the amount of sugar in your body) to stay healthy. Symptoms include frequent urination, excessive thirst, unusual weight loss, blurred vision and the disease can sometimes be fatal. People with diabetes excrete sugar in their urine – in the old days doctors tested for the condition by tasting the urine of patients to see if it was sweet!

Diabetes used to be treated with insulin extracted from the glands of cows (and later pigs), but this was a limited source and sometimes the patient's body rejected the insulin. Nowadays, scientists can produce human insulin by inserting the 'genetic instruction' that causes human cells to make insulin into the DNA strands of bacteria cells. These cells are then given a good supply of oxygen and food and the bacteria begin to make human insulin

▲ In this factory, yeast is genetically engineered to make insulin for the treatment of diabetes. The yeast is fermented in these large metal containers.

themselves. This type of insulin is more compatible with the human body and can be made in unlimited supplies. It can also be produced in a very short time, because the bacteria grow and multiply so quickly.

▲ Scientists are continuing to search for new ways in which bacteria can be used in our everyday lives.

6

The multiple life

Multi-celled organisms, like plants and animals, are composed of many cells that perform a particular function. These larger organisms have developed clever transport systems that enable them to supply all cells with the substances they need to carry out the processes of life. This impressive co-operation of cells enables multi-celled organisms to undertake a vast collection of different processes.

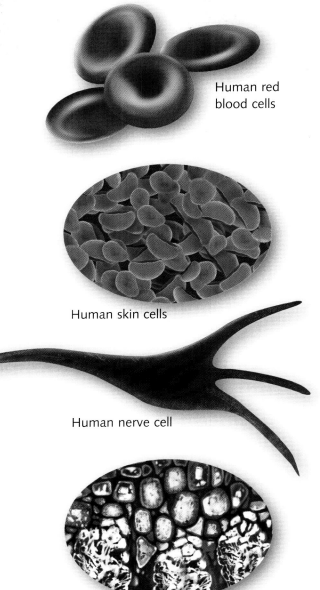

Human red blood cells

Human skin cells

Human nerve cell

Human bone cells

ANIMAL MULTI-CELLED ORGANISMS

Multi-celled organisms can have cells of the same or of different types. More complex life forms are made from a variety of different cells – there are over 200 types of cells in the human body, for example.

Often cells with a common structure and function will form a group in order to do a particular job. These groups are called 'tissues' (such as skin tissue or muscle tissue). Likewise, tissues may group together to make 'organs' that are designed to perform a specific function (such as the eyes, lungs or kidneys). Organs in turn may group together to carry out a task. We call this an 'organ system' (such as the digestive system or the circulatory system).

In multi-celled organisms, life processes are carried out through different cell groupings that make tissues and organs. For example:

▶ Movement is carried out when muscle tissues are attached to bone tissue, and work together.

▶ Respiration occurs in all cells and the ingredients required (oxygen and food) are transported by the circulatory (blood) system.

▶ Nutrients are gathered by the digestive system while the kidneys, lungs and skin cells control excretion.

INVESTIGATE

▶ Look up as many human cell types as you can find (there are over 200!).

▶ Research the names of the different organs that make up the human digestive system.

► Growth occurs as all cells grow, divide and eventually become replaced. The specialised organs and cells of the reproductive system also work together to create new living organisms.

► Sensitivity is found in cells like those in the fingertips.

These tissues and organs are discussed in more detail on page 35.

PLANT MULTI-CELLED ORGANISMS

Like animals, plants are also multi-celled. Their cells group together to form tissues and organs that carry out specific jobs. Plant organs include the roots, leaves, flowers and fruit. For example, cells in the leaves work together to make food in the process of photosynthesis (see page 9).

SINGLE-CELLED OR MULTI-CELLED?

Sometimes it is difficult to tell whether more unusual organisms are single-celled or multi-celled – or indeed, how they carry out the processes of life at all. For each of the following living organisms, use what you have learnt so far, together with the information given below, to decide whether you believe the organism is single-celled or multi-celled. Write down the reasons for your decision and what factors might have changed your mind.

ORGANISM 1 MOULD

Moulds are a type of fungi and are close in structure to mushrooms and toadstools. Moulds are mostly visible to the naked eye, but other parts of their delicate structure can only be seen with the aid of a microscope. Most moulds are shaped like filaments and this helps them to invade solid substances such as bread and fruit (above right).

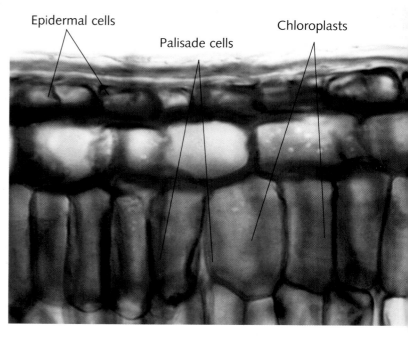

Epidermal cells   Palisade cells   Chloroplasts

▲ These stained holly leaf cells, viewed under a light microscope (x 490 magnification) show the different cells, and cell components, that help leaves to function.

The cells do not contain chlorophyll so the process of photosynthesis does not occur. The structure of mould is divided into cells and many nuclei are found in the cytoplasm.

Organism 2 Yeast

Yeast is another fungus that has been used for a long time in brewing and baking. In baking, yeast cells feed off the sugar in a bread mixture. They produce carbon dioxide which, when released, causes the bread to rise. Yeast cells are round. As they grow, yeast cells extend sections (called buds) that enlarge and eventually become detached, to lead to new cells.

▲ Yeast cell

DID YOU KNOW?

▶ Some slime mould can be single-celled or multi-celled. Most of the time slime mould lives as a single-celled organism that looks rather like an amoeba. However, in difficult conditions – such as when food is in short supply – thousands of individual slime mould cells come together to form a multi-celled organism, which scientists call a 'slug'. This enables the slime mould cells to move to where living conditions are more favourable.

Organism 4 Spirogyras

Spirogyras are a form of algae that can be found in ponds; they look like green slime. This organism grows so well that by the end of the summer there can be a thick scum on the surface of water. Spirogyras contain chloroplasts that run through the middle of the organism as a spiral. However, unlike other plants, spirogyras do not have stems, leaves and roots.

▼ Spirogyras

▼ Paramecia

Organism 3 Paramecia

Paramecia are organisms that live in water or other cells. They have a stiff outer coating that gives them a permanent shape. Paramecia swim rapidly by waving hair-like projections called cilia that help to propel them forward. Paramecia contain a nucleus and some have a cell wall. Others have chloroplasts, allowing them to feed like a plant.

Organism 5 Diatoms

Diatoms are organisms that have chloroplasts that enable them to photosynthesise. They have cell walls that are mostly pen-shaped. Diatoms are found mostly in fresh water and they can be caught with fine mesh nets. Diatoms form colonies in long chains. Diatoms can only be seen under a microscope.

▶ Diatom

Specialised cells

7

Although a number of different cells work together to sustain the life of a multi-celled organism, some cells are more special than others. It is thanks to specialised cells, that plants and animals are able to carry out some of the more complicated processes of life.

SPECIAL ANIMAL CELLS

All animal cells respire and need to work together in order to maintain a steady supply of oxygen and nutrients around the body. But some animal cells also carry out very particular jobs.

DID YOU KNOW?

▶ The electric eel is capable of storing up to 650 volts of electricity in its nerve cells. The eel uses this electricity to stun its prey. It also uses it to help with navigation – when the eel approaches an object its electric field changes.

Cell	Image	Function	Description
Red blood cells		Carry oxygen to all parts of the body.	Contain a substance called 'haemoglobin' that carries oxygen. Red blood cells do not have a nucleus so that there is more room for oxygen to be carried. They are quite flexible so that they can fit through narrow blood vessels.
Nerve cells		Carry nerve impulses to all parts of the body.	Very long cells that can carry electric impulses. An insulating substance called the 'sheath' surrounds each cell. The cells have branching ends that connect to other cells passing electric impulses quite easily.
Sperm cells		Carry male genetic information and join to egg cell in sexual reproduction.	Contain a tail that allows the cell to swim to the female egg cell so that **fertilisation** can occur. The head of the cell contains genetic information and chemicals that penetrate the egg cell.

SPECIAL PLANT CELLS

Like animals, plants also need specialist cells to carry out some of the more complicated processes of life.

INVESTIGATE

▶ Do some research in other books and on the internet to see if you can find what makes the following cells specialised and what the functions of these cells are.

(1) Muscle cell
(2) Egg cell
(3) Stem cell
(4) Xylem cell

Cell	Image	Function	Description
Palisade cells		Turn light from the Sun into food (glucose) for the plant. This process is called photosynthesis.	Tall columns found near the surface of a leaf so that they are as close to the Sun as possible. Contain chloroplasts filled with chlorophyll that the plant needs for food production.
Epidermal cells		Prevent the leaf from losing too much water and drying out.	Form a waterproof layer across the top of leaves. The cells are spread thinly so that sunlight can pass through them.
Guard cells		Allow gases needed for respiration to pass into and out of the leaf.	Surround the pores of leaves on their bottom surface. The cells help to regulate the rate of gas exchange by becoming turgid or flaccid, depending on how much water they contain. When a lot of water is present, the guard cells swell, helping to open the pores.

TIME TRAVEL: INTO THE FUTURE

Cells that have not grown into any specialist cell type are called 'stem cells'. Every single cell in your body 'stems' (originates) from this type of cell. Stem cells are found in early embryos but scientists have recently begun to find them also in adult bone and skin tissue. Scientists are looking at how stem cells might be used to restore tissues that have been damaged by injury or disease. For example, transplanting stem cells into damaged areas might encourage the stem cells to specialise and grow new, healthy tissues.

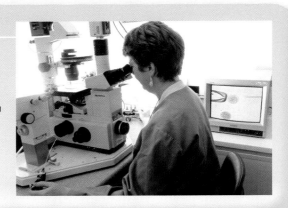

TISSUES

Specialised cells cannot do much on their own but group them together and they spring into action – compare a single red blood cell to a group of blood cells that carry all the oxygen that the body needs. Tissues are formed in multi-celled organisms by groups of similar cells working together.

In plants, vascular tissue allows materials (such as food substances) to pass through the plant's structure (see page 41). A series of vascular cells are grouped together throughout the plant – if plants had only one vascular cell, food substances wouldn't get very far!

ORGANS

The heart that pumps blood around your body is made up of muscle tissue, nerve tissue and blood tissue. Tissues cannot always perform complex jobs on their own so they group together to form an organ. Plants have organs too. For example, flowers are made up from different tissues like the carpel and stamen, that work together to attract insects to the plant. Other plant organs include roots, stems and leaves.

ORGAN SYSTEMS

Some jobs are just too big and complex to be done by a single organ. Groups of organs work together to form an 'organ system' so that these more difficult jobs can be carried out. In humans and animals, the digestive system includes the stomach, liver and intestines. The stomach concentrates on breaking down food into smaller parts, the liver filters out waste material and the intestines are responsible for absorbing the good parts of food that our bodies need.

The cells, tissues and organs of your body work together to keep your body healthy. Your body temperature is regulated by the skin, muscle, nervous and circulatory systems working together. Levels of water are also controlled by processes such as thirst and urination.

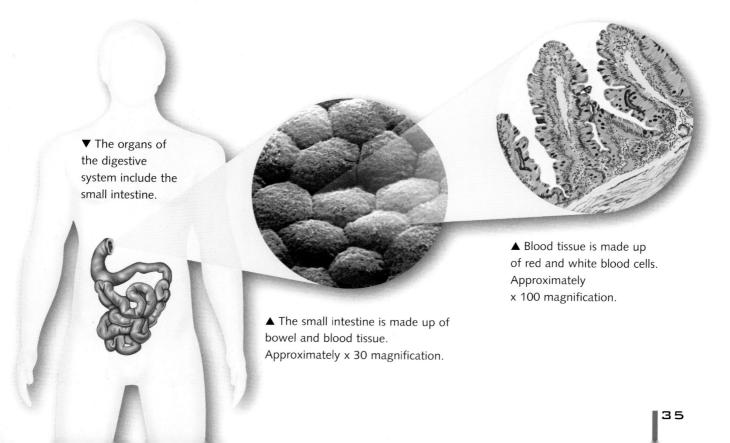

▼ The organs of the digestive system include the small intestine.

▲ The small intestine is made up of bowel and blood tissue. Approximately x 30 magnification.

▲ Blood tissue is made up of red and white blood cells. Approximately x 100 magnification.

8

Animal organ systems

Planet Earth is now inhabited by billions of different animal species. Although these creatures take many different forms, their bodies are kept in good working order thanks to the creative design of their organ systems. These systems are made up of cells, tissues and individual organs that all work together to sustain life.

BONES OF THE SKELETAL SYSTEM

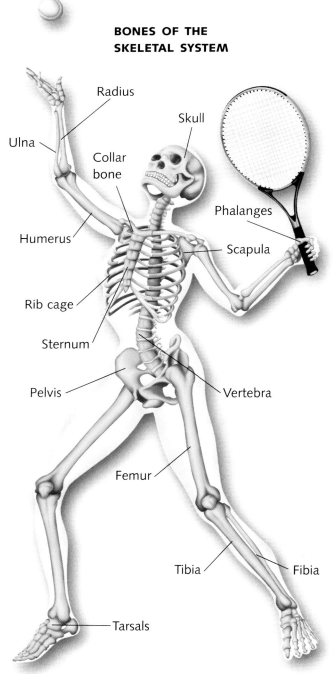

Radius

Skull

Ulna

Collar bone

Humerus

Phalanges

Scapula

Rib cage

Sternum

Pelvis

Vertebra

Femur

Tibia

Fibia

Tarsals

SKELETAL AND MUSCLE SYSTEMS

Animals are able to move because their skeleton and muscles work together. These organs make up an organ system. Although our skeletons are used for support and protection they are also attached to our muscles to ease movement. When we move, our muscles contract and relax, enabling our limbs to change position. Different organisms have muscles that move in different ways. For example, snakes and fish move their bodies from side to side because their muscles contract and relax together in set patterns.

MUSCLES OF THE MUSCLE SYSTEM

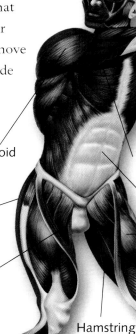

Biceps

Pectoralis

Triceps

Abdominals

Deltoid

Gluteus maximus

Quadriceps

Adductors

Sartorius

Tibialis anterior

Hamstring

Gastrocnemius

Achilles' tendon

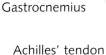

NERVOUS SYSTEM

The main organs of the nervous system are the brain, spinal cord and nervous tissue running throughout the body. Animals need to be sensitive to their environment so that they can respond to danger. Sensitive cells pick up a stimulus and send messages to the brain via nerve cells. The brain in turn sends messages to the nerve cells that control the muscles, causing them to move. For example, if your hand touches something hot, cells in your fingers send messages to the brain, which tell you to move your hand away quickly! This process happens extremely fast and we often move without actually thinking about it.

PARTS OF THE NERVOUS SYSTEM

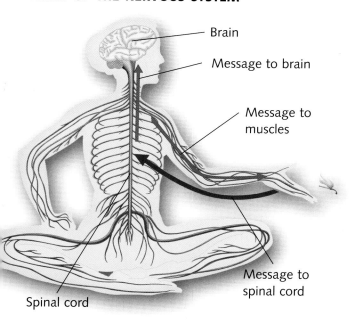

Brain

Message to brain

Message to muscles

Message to spinal cord

Spinal cord

ENDOCRINE SYSTEM

This system consists of all the **glands** throughout the body that are responsible for secreting chemicals called **hormones** that make changes to our bodies over time. Our glands are constantly releasing hormones that travel to the parts of the body where they are needed through the blood system. The glands of the endocrine system are found in the brain, pancreas and ovaries or testes.

For example, the endocrine system secretes a growth hormone from a gland found in the brain called the pituitary gland. Hormones travel through the blood system in the plasma. As they do not travel through nerve cells, their journey takes a little longer.

CIRCULATORY SYSTEM

The blood plays a role in all processes of life and is an essential transport mechanism. The blood system is made up of arteries, capillaries and veins. Through these vessels all blood cells travel and carry out their important work around the body. Blood also plays an important role in healing. When we cut ourselves, we bleed and our blood reacts to being exposed to the air and starts to clot. White blood cells are also a vital tool in the fight against infection.

RESPIRATORY SYSTEM

The main organs of the respiratory system are the lungs (for animals that live on land). The lungs are designed to allow oxygen to be taken in and carbon dioxide to be released from the body. Oxygen is required for respiration and is transported from the lungs (via the bloodstream) to all the cells of a living organism. Respiration produces carbon dioxide and because this gas can be poisonous it travels back to the lungs through the blood to be breathed out. Oxygen and carbon dioxide travel to and from the lungs (an organ) in the blood cells (cells) of the blood vessels (tissues). Animals that live in water have developed different organs through which they can exchange the gases oxygen and carbon dioxide. Fish have 'gills', which extract oxygen from water as it flows over them, and release carbon dioxide.

DIGESTIVE SYSTEM

The digestive system is responsible for allowing organisms to feed and is also where food is processed and broken down. The organs of the human digestive system carry out specific functions and include the mouth, the oesophagus (food pipe), the stomach and the intestines. As food passes through each of these organs it becomes a little closer to being fully broken down. When it is completely broken down, food is absorbed into the cells and is used for the process of respiration and for building new cells. Following respiration, the cells release waste products into the blood to be transported to parts of the body where they can be excreted.

Some animals, such as cows, have stomachs that are made up from at least four compartments. This is because these animals feed on a large amount of grass, which takes longer to be broken down. The four compartments are necessary to allow full breakdown to occur. Cows also have special bacteria in their gut that help to break down the cellulose (fibre) in grass.

▲ Cows have four compartments in their stomach that help them to digest the tough grass that they eat.

PARTS OF THE DIGESTIVE SYSTEM

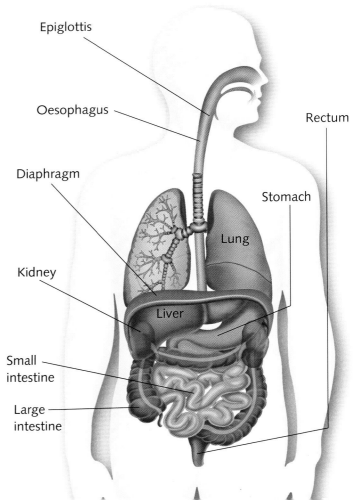

Epiglottis

Oesophagus

Rectum

Diaphragm

Stomach

Lung

Kidney

Liver

Small intestine

Large intestine

Male

Female

▼ The male reproductive organs include the testes and the penis.

▼ The female reproductive organs include the ovaries, oviducts and uterus.

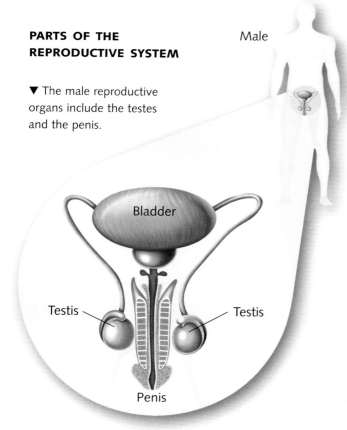

Bladder

Testis

Testis

Penis

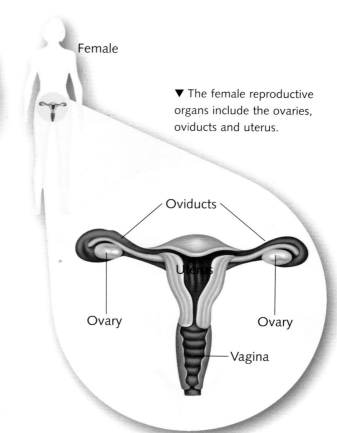

Oviducts

Uterus

Ovary

Ovary

Vagina

REPRODUCTIVE SYSTEM

The main organs of this system are the testes and penis (for men) and ovaries, oviducts and uterus (for women). Hormones released in the endocrine system (see page 37) control both of these systems, and the changes that occur can often be complicated and difficult to understand. The purpose of the reproductive system is to create new individuals that are capable of carrying out the processes of life on their own. A sperm cell from the male fuses with an egg cell from the female to make a single cell that grows, divides and multiplies. It is incredible to think that we all started as a single cell which has now developed individual tissues and organs!

EXCRETORY SYSTEM

The main organs of the excretory system are the large intestines, skin, lungs, kidney and bladder. Excretion involves getting rid of waste products that would otherwise be harmful to our bodies.

TEST YOURSELF

▶ Using your knowledge of animal organs, state which organ systems are involved in the following changes:

(1) Moving our hands from a hot stove

(2) Changing from a child into an adult

(3) Breaking down a cheese sandwich after eating it

(4) Walking the dog

(5) Playing in a football match

(6) Sweating

When cells release these products, they pass into tissues and travel through the blood to parts of the body where they can be excreted. Undigested food also passes through the digestive system. Excretion occurs in the form of urine, feaces, salt, and sweat, and carbon dioxide that is breathed out.

9

Plant organ systems

It is estimated that there are at least 260,000 species of plants in the world today, from small mosses to tall trees. Although plants don't move from place to place like animals, special organ systems help to keep them thriving. Next time you look at a plant, take a thought for all the work that's going on!

ABSORPTIVE SYSTEM

Plants are heavily dependent on water to carry out the processes of life. Plant cells become turgid when they absorb water, giving the plant an essential support structure. Plants also need water to grow. Roots form the main organ of the absorptive system – absorbing water from the soil after rainfall. Roots have a very particular shape that helps them to grow through soil and between rocks in search of water. Sometimes the roots can even support a plant that grows on a cliff face. Fine hairs on the surface of the roots have a large surface area to volume ratio so that water can pass into the root quite easily.

The root organ system has adapted to cover as much ground as possible. Roots can grow in all directions in search of water. The strength of some tree roots can crack pavements and buildings. Roots grow in a branched way so that they can also double as support for a plant.

▶ Plant roots have hairs at the tip that absorb water from the soil so that it can be transported to the plant's leaves.

PLANT TISSUES AND ORGANS SYSTEMS

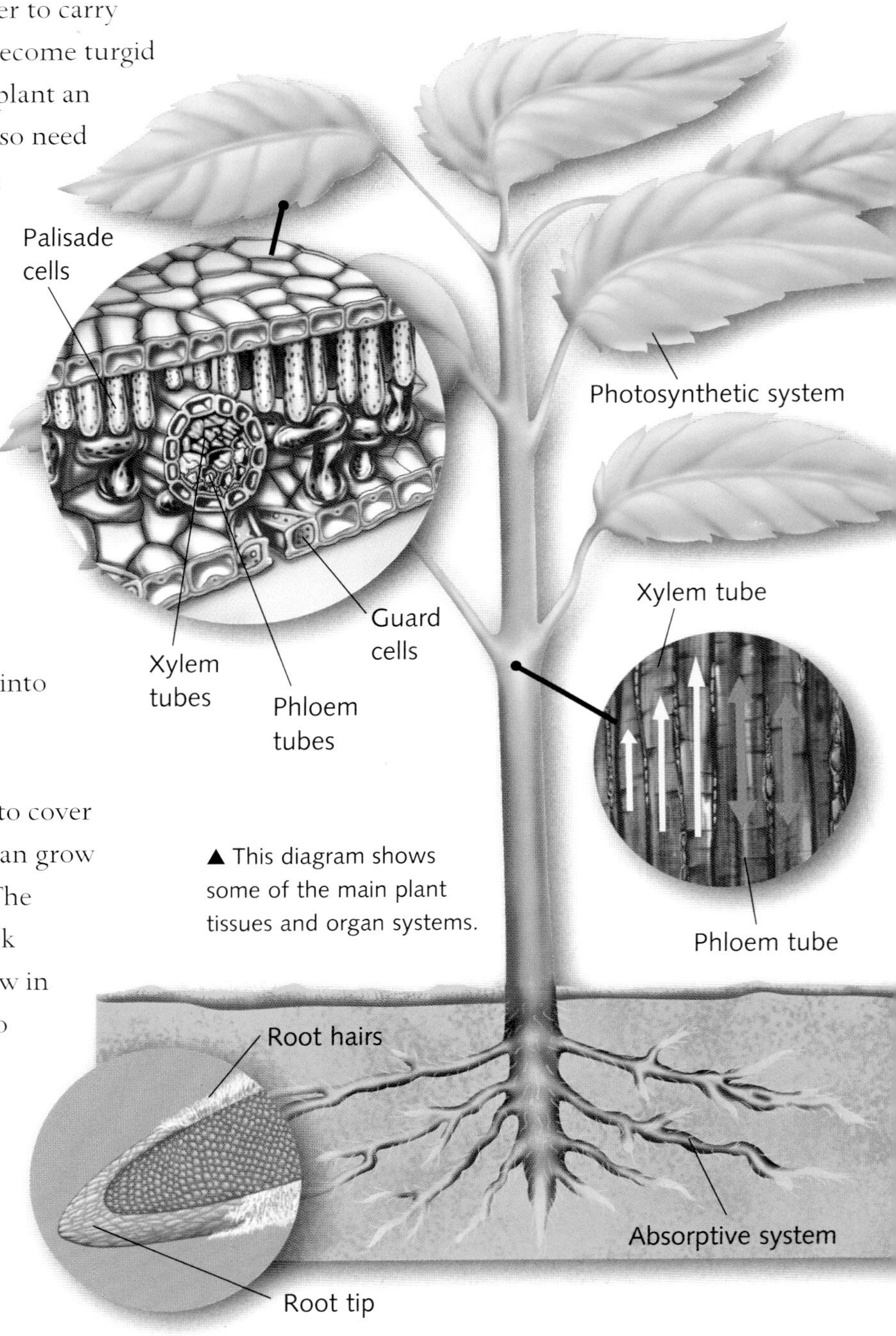

Palisade cells

Photosynthetic system

Xylem tubes

Guard cells

Phloem tubes

Xylem tube

Phloem tube

▲ This diagram shows some of the main plant tissues and organ systems.

Root hairs

Absorptive system

Root tip

VASCULAR SYSTEM

This system is made up of the stem (an organ) and the tissues found inside the stem — most notably the 'xylem' and the 'phloem' vessels. These tissues are composed of individual cells that line up alongside each other to form tubes through the stem. The xylem vessels are responsible for allowing water to pass from the roots of a plant to the stem, and later to the leaves where they are needed. The phloem vessels allow the transport of food from the leaves to the rest of the plant. Together these two tissues support all the processes of life.

The stem also has another very important role in the plant. Xylem and phloem vessels are very strong and are capable of supporting the whole plant. The stem can also rotate so that leaves can be held in the best position for photosynthesis (see page 9) and flowers in the best position for **pollination** (see page 42).

PHOTOSYNTHETIC SYSTEM

Plants make their own food, called glucose, by the process of photosynthesis. During this process they need light, carbon dioxide and water. Light and carbon dioxide are taken into the plant through the leaves. Water passes into the plant from the soil via the roots and the stem. The main organ of the photosynthetic system is the leaf.

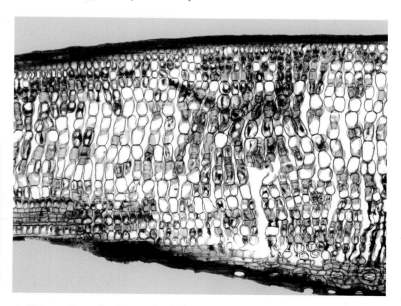

▲ This section of a Spruce leaf, shows the tightly packed palisade cells that are used in photosynthesis. Light microscope image x 70 magnification.

Leaves are made up from many types of tissues, but the ones that are important for photosynthesis are called the palisade tissue and the spongy tissue. Palisade tissue contains cells that have chloroplasts in them. These cells are arranged in a line at the top of the leaf to make it easy for sunlight to be captured and used for photosynthesis.

Spongy tissue is made up from spongy cells arranged randomly so that there are lots of air spaces between them. These air spaces are very important to let carbon dioxide travel into the plant and the waste product of oxygen to pass out. As the cells are not packed too tightly together, there is plenty of space for the two gases to be exchanged.

Once a plant has gained glucose from photosynthesis, it can carry out the process of respiration. Like animals, plants use respiration to make the energy that they need to perform other life processes (see page 6).

REPRODUCTIVE SYSTEM

In plants, the reproductive system uses a number of organs to create new individuals. These organs include flowers and fruits, which are present at different parts of a plant's reproductive cycle.

Some plants have particularly colourful and fragrant flowers. This helps these plants to attract insects for pollination – when bees feed on

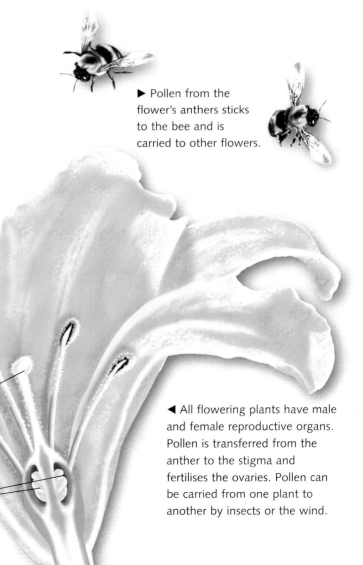

▶ Pollen from the flower's anthers sticks to the bee and is carried to other flowers.

PARTS OF THE REPRODUCTIVE SYSTEM

Petal

Anther

Stigma

Ovaries

◀ All flowering plants have male and female reproductive organs. Pollen is transferred from the anther to the stigma and fertilises the ovaries. Pollen can be carried from one plant to another by insects or the wind.

flowers, pollen sticks to their backs and later gets transferred to another flower. Pollination is the process by which the sex cells of one flower meet the sex cells of another so that reproduction can occur. Many plants rely on insects to carry pollen from one place to another, while other plants rely on the wind to carry their sex cells.

▲ This star mushroom is spreading its spores to reproduce. Mushrooms (and other fungi) are non-flowering plants. The mushroom that is visible is like the fruit of other plants. The rest of the plant is hidden below the soil.

▼ Monkeys help plants to reproduce by eating their fruit and spreading the seeds in their faeces.

Once pollination has occurred, flowers turn to fruits, which are other organs of the reproductive system. Fruits contain seeds, which are capable of growing into new individuals. Fruits have a sweet taste, encouraging animals to eat them and later spread the fruit's seeds through their faeces.

10

Time travel: The origins of life

Scientific studies have shown that life hasn't always existed on Earth. So what type of cell could have kick-started the diverse range of living things now inhabiting our planet? Many scientists believe that the first living organism was 'single-celled' and similar in many ways to bacteria. But if this is true, how did such a living organism come to develop?

The right conditions

Most scientists believe that life started from a mixture of materials present in ancient times. In 1871, the scientist Charles Darwin suggested that life began in a 'warm little pond' where energy and a number of chemicals combined to form the first living organism. Later in the 1950s, Harold Urey and his graduate student Stanley Miller (at the University of Chicago) began to examine what kind of environment would be necessary for life to begin. In 1953, they conducted an experiment that had a huge influence on future investigations into the origins of life.

Miller filled a glass container with water and several gases that he thought were present in the atmosphere of early Earth – methane, ammonia, hydrogen and water from volcanic activity. He then ran an electrical charge through the material, in an attempt to recreate the lightning storms that were thought to be common on Earth at this time. After a week, Miller found that his chemicals had reacted to form a number of organic compounds. These are compounds that contain carbon and are believed to be essential to cellular life. All living things on Earth are based on carbon.

Although some scientists criticise the work of Miller and Urey, their experiment is still considered to be an extremely important landmark in cellular biology because it showed that organic compounds could be produced from simple chemicals, combined with an energy source such as lightning. This groundbreaking research led scientists to become very optimistic that the mysteries of life's origin would be solved within a few decades. But today, it seems that the investigations have only just begun!

▼ A scientist adjusts equipment during a demonstration of the Miller-Urey experiment into the origins of life.

ORIGINS IN SPACE

Scientists now know that the organic compounds made in the Miller/Urey experiment can be found in outer space. Similar substances have been found in the remains of meteorites – rocks from outer space that have crashed into the Earth. This suggests that a series of comets or asteroids may have brought these substances of life to planet Earth. Some argue that if the substances of life can survive the extreme conditions of outer space, perhaps they were present when the Earth actually formed. Others say that – even if this were the case – there would not be enough material to create the large collection of life that has arisen on our planet. One important result of these space theories is that perhaps the substances of life are widely spread throughout space but only come to life on planets, like Earth, that have the right environmental conditions that suit living things.

A GENETIC FOUNDATION

All living organisms have a genetic code found within the DNA of their cells (see page 14). In the last ten years, scientists working for the International Human Genome Project and other privately-funded groups have been working hard to uncover the genetic codes of a variety of organisms. These codes determine the design of an organism and the processes needed to keep it alive, but they are also an important historical record of the development of an organism. If two organisms have genetic similarities they are very likely to have arisen from a

common ancestor. Fossil evidence has previously been the only way that we could begin to compile a 'family tree' of life on Earth. By comparing genetic codes, scientists can now begin to redefine this family tree and perhaps eventually discover life's origins.

Another mystery that scientists are trying to solve is whether genetic material or cells came first – DNA contains instructions that make cells work, but DNA also needs cells to reproduce. In 1983, US scientists Sidney Altman and Thomas Cech added a possible solution to this problem when they found that **RNA** (a substance that acts like part of a cell, but also carries genetic information) could also encourage chemical reactions within a cell. Altman and Cech shared the 1989 Nobel Prize in Chemistry for their discovery – perhaps their finding also holds the key to the first building block of life?

▶ **Comets or asteroids may have brought substances of life to planet Earth.**

DID YOU KNOW?

▶ It is thought that all life on Earth descended from a single-celled organism that lived about 3.5 billion years ago. Scientists have been looking at the sequence of DNA in genes to try to trace this original organism. They have found, for example, that many genes perform the same role in human cells and in bacterial cells, suggesting that they originate from a common ancestor.

Glossary

AEROBIC BACTERIA – Bacteria that respire using oxygen.

AQUATIC – Living and growing on or in water.

ASEXUAL – Reproduction that occurs without the use of sex cells.

BINARY FISSION – A type of asexual reproduction that involves the splitting of a parent cell into two approximately equal parts.

BIOFILM – A group of micro-organisms that are usually joined together and attached to a solid surface.

CYANOBACTERIA – Bacteria that gain their energy through photosynthesis.

DNA (DEOXYRIBONUCLEIC ACID) – A substance in the nucleus of each living cell that holds all the inherited characteristics of the plant or animal.

ECOSYSTEM – A collection of living things and the environment in which they live.

ENZYMES – Substances found in living things that speed up the rate of biological reactions.

EUKARYOTES – Single-celled or multi-celled organisms whose cells contain a nucleus.

EXTREMOPHILE – An organism that lives under extreme environmental conditions.

FERTILISATION – The joining together of male and female reproductive cells to start the growth of a new organism. The ova (egg cells) in flowers are fertilised by the male pollen cells. The eggs cells in animals are fertilised by the male sperm cells.

FLACCID – Lacking in stiffness or firmness.

GENE – A short piece of DNA which is the code for a particular characteristic. The study of genes is called genetics.

GLANDS – A group of cells that produce special chemicals, called hormones, that the body can use or excrete.

ANSWERS

p7 Test yourself
Emu: movement by running; respiration by breathing; sensitivity by seeing predators; growth by growing with age; reproduction by laying eggs following fertilisation; excretion by releasing waste products; nutrition by feeding on plant and seed matter. Water lily: movement by growing and opening / closing flowers; respiration during the process of photosynthesis; sensitivity by detecting sunlight and opening and closing flowers; growth of stems, leaves and flowers; reproduction by making seeds and sprouting new plants from roots; excretion by releasing waste products through leaves and roots; nutrition by absorbing nutrients through roots and by making food during photosynthesis.

p9 Test yourself
Examples could include: Spinal cord – sensitive to signals from all other nerve cells. Used to send all messages to the brain. Nostrils – sensitive to smells and used to send information about smells to the brain. Ears – sensitive to sound waves and used to send information about sounds to the brain. Brain – sensitive to all signals. The brain processes these into signals for muscles to act upon.

p13 Investigate
Size of cell = measured size / magnification.
(1) real size approximately 0.16 mm x 0.05 mm
(2) real size approximately 0.03 mm x 0.03 mm

p15 Test yourself
Cell wall, vacuole, chloroplasts. The plant would collapse without any support; the plant would be unable to store water and vital nutrients; the plant would be unable to photosynthesise to make food and would eventually starve to death.

p17 Test yourself
Cell 1: surface area = 60 cm^2 / volume = 24 cm^3 / ratio = 60:24 (2.5:1). Cell 2: surface area = 54 cm^2 / volume = 27 cm^3 / ratio = 54:27 (2:1). Cell 3: surface area = 10 cm^2 / volume = 2 cm^3 / ratio = 10:2 (5:1). Cell 3 would find it easiest to satisfy food and oxygen needs because it has the largest 'surface area to volume ratio'.

p19 Test yourself
Barnacles – can move which is one life process; they also feed. Venus Flytrap – can move which is one life process. Although they are plants, they can also eat an animal organism.

p27 Test yourself
Bacteria – (4 of the following) single-celled, variety of shapes and sizes, no nucleus but contain strands of DNA, some have hair strands called flagella, divide

HORMONES – Chemical substances produced by the body by glands that are transported by the blood to other organs to stimulate their function. Hormones are chemical messengers.

HOST CELL – A cell in which a parasite lives.

NUTRIENT – Any substance that is nourishing or provides food for a living organism.

ORGANISM – A living animal or plant.

PHOTOSYNTHESIS – The process in green plants in which foods (mainly sugars) are made from carbon dioxide and water, using energy from the sunlight.

POLLINATION – The transfer of pollen grains from the male anther to the female stigma in flowering plants.

PROKARYOTES – Single-celled organisms whose cells do not contain a nucleus.

REPRODUCTION – The sexual or asexual process by which living organisms produce offspring.

RESPIRE – The process of releasing energy from food.

RNA (RIBONUCLEIC ACID) – A long molecule, similar to DNA. RNA carries the information from DNA in the cell's nucleus to the body of the cell and uses the genetic information to make proteins.

SEEDS – A ripe, fertilised female reproductive cell that will develop into a new plant under suitable conditions.

TENTACLES – A long, flexible part of an organ that extends.

TURGID – Swollen or filled with fluid.

VACUOLE – A small cavity in the cytoplasm of a cell, surrounded by a single membrane and containing water, food or waste material.

Useful websites:
www.bbc.co.uk/schools
www.nationalgeographic.com
www.sciencenewsforkids.org
www.newscientist.com
www.howstuffworks.com

using binary fission. Viruses – (4 of the following) not cells themselves but parasites on a host cell, variety of shapes and sizes but most can only be viewed using an electron microscope, can be harmful to the host cell, capable of sensitivity, reproduce by injecting genetic information into the cytoplasm of a host cell.

p30 Investigate
(2) The human digestive system is made up of mouth, oesophagus (food pipe), stomach, liver, pancreas, gall bladder, kidneys, intestines.

p31/32 Test yourself paragraph
Organism 1 multi-celled. Organism 2 single-celled. Organism 3 single-celled. Organism 4 multi-celled. Organism 5 single-celled.

p34 Investigate
(1) Has long strips of fibres (striated) to allow contraction during movement. (2) Contains only half the genetic content of all other cells. Fuses with a sperm cell to create another organism. (3) Not specialised in any way! Can be made into any other type of cell. (4) Tube-like cells in plants that line up to allow water to pass through them.

p37 Test yourself
Brain – nervous system; Spinal cord – nervous system; Nerves – nervous system; Eye – nervous system; Heart – circulatory system; Blood – circulatory system; Lungs – respiratory and excretory systems; Stomach – digestive system; Liver – digestive and circulatory systems; Pancreas – digestive and endocrine systems; Intestines – digestive and excretory systems; Kidneys – excretory system; Skin – excretory system; Glands – endocrine system; Bones – skeletal and muscle systems; Muscles – skeletal and muscle systems; Ovaries – reproductive system; Testes – reproductive system.

p39 Test yourself
(1) Nervous system, skeletal and muscle systems. (2) Endocrine system. (3) Digestive system. (4) Skeletal and muscle systems. (5) Skeletal and muscle systems. (6) Excretory system.

p42 Investigate
Example answer – The eye is a collection of light-sensitive cells that have grouped together. This organ does not have blood flowing through it so we can see clearly. We have two eyes to help us to judge distances more accurately (binocular vision). Our pupils adjust to allow different amounts of light into our eyes.

p43 Test yourself
Example answers – Flowering plants are insect-pollinated; water plants are water-pollinated; fruit trees rely on animals to transport their seeds; some fruit trees have been bred to become self-pollinating.

Index

PHOTO CREDITS – *(abbv: r, right, l, left, t, top, m, middle, b, bottom)* **Cover background image** Steve Gschmeissner/Science Photo Library **Front cover images** (r) Mike Hill/Oxford Scientific (l) Dr Yorgos Nikas/Science Photo Library **Back cover image** (inset) Mike Hill/Oxford Scientific **p.1** (tr) Steve Gschmeissner/Science Photo Library (bl) www.istockphoto.com/Jody Elliott (br) www.istockphoto.com/Chris Schmidt **p.2** (bl) www.istockphoto.com /Edward Karaa **p.3** (tr) www.istockphoto.com/Andrea Gingerich (br) Colin Cuthbert/Science Photo Library **p.4** (tl) Adam Hart-Davis/Science Photo Library (tr) www.istockphoto.com/Monika Wisniewska (br) www.istockphoto.com/Michael Chen **p.5** Russel Kightley/Science Photo Library **p.6** (t) Tim Davis/Science Photo Library (b) www.istockphoto.com/ Gerald Klassen **p.7** www.istockphoto.com/Zenz Sonnema **p.8** (both) Adam Hart-Davis/Science Photo Library **p.11** (t) Dr Jeremy Burgess/Science Photo Library (b) Chris Knapton/Science Photo Library **p.13** (tr) M.I. Walker/Science Photo Library (ml) Colin Cuthbert/Science Photo Library (mr) Dee Breger/Science Photo Library (b) Science Photo Library **p.14** www.istockphoto.com/Michael Chen **p.15** Hybrid Medical Animation /Science Photo Library **p.19** (tr) Camr/A.B Dowsett/Science Photo Library (bm) Barrie Watts/Oxford Scientific (br) www.istockphoto.com/Thomas Mounsey **p.20** (tr) www.istockphoto.com/Sampsa Kaijaluoto **p.21** Hybrid Medical Animation/Science Photo Library **p.22** Astrid & Hanns Frieder Michler/Science Photo Library **p.25** (t) CNRI/Science Photo Library (b) www.istockphoto.com/Ben Renard-Wlart **p.26** Russel Kightley/Science Photo Library **p.27** (t) Science Photo Library (b) Simon Fraser/Science Photo Library **p.28** (r) www.istockphoto.com (l) www.istockphoto.com/Jody Elliott **p.29** (t) Volker Steger/Science Photo Library (b) Sinclair Stammers/Science Photo Library **p.31** (t) Claude Nuridsany & Marie Perennou/Science Photo Library (b) www.istockphoto.com/Krzysztof Niedecki **p.33** (t) www.istockphoto.com/Monika Wisniewska (m) Michael Abbey/Science Photo Library (b) Steve Gschmeissner/Science Photo Library **p.34** (tl) Alfred Pasieka/Science Photo Library (ml) M.I. Walker/Science Photo Library (bl) Dr Jeremy Burgess/Science Photo Library (b) James King-Holmes/Science Photo Library **p.38** www.istockphoto.com/Chris Schmidt **p.41** (t) www.istockphoto.com/Andrea Gingerich (b) Alfred Pasieka/Science Photo Library **p.43** (l) Jeff Lepore/Science Photo Library (r) www.istockphoto.com/Edward Karaa **p.44** Peter Menzel/Science Photo Library **p.45** Tony & Daphne Hallas/Science Photo Library.